The unbreakable mind

Overcoming Anxiety, stress and overthinking

Peter E.Coyne

Table of contents

Introduction

Anxiety can make life seem like a nightmare that you are awake from. It's as though everything you think, feel, and do is shrouded in unfavorable thinking. With ever-increasing limitations that make it challenging to be spontaneous or relaxed, life can sometimes feel claustrophobic. The worst part is that you and those around you might not even comprehend why any of it is occurring. It could feel as though people are trying to make sense of your worry by blaming it on your attitude, calling you too sensitive, or just expecting you to get over it because they've carefully outlined all the reasons why your anxieties are illogical. Nevertheless, nothing is ever that easy, is it? In this book, we'll look more closely at what anxiety is, how it functions, and how you may learn to manage your anxiety while still leading a fulfilling life. Overthinking under stress might seem like a catch, something you can never get out of or solve. You can, though! This book is a terrific place to start if you're ready to make a sincere change, take care of yourself, and take some decisive first steps toward a life with less anxiety.

First things first: you are not wrong, stupid, or crazy. Anxiety is a real psychological phenomenon. And just because you haven't found out how to overcome worry doesn't make you a horrible person. Letting go of the habit of self-criticism, self-blame, or feeling humiliated about how you are feeling is one of the first steps to healing from anxiety.

While you are now responsible for your anxiety, it is not your fault. I'm trying to say that even though you didn't choose to have anxiety, you always have the option to take the necessary steps to escape its grip.

If you've come to the point in your life when you feel as though anxiety is holding you hostage and won't let go, this book is for you.

The strange thing about anxiety is that, despite your best efforts to maintain control, you feel more helpless than ever and completely at the whim of intense, uncontrollable emotions. Many of us have a preconceived notion of what "anxiety" looks like, but this notion is more expensive than you may think.

In our professional lives, anxiety can manifest as self-doubt, imposter syndrome, or burnout. It might get in the way of our connections with the people we care about. It might be waiting for us in the background, prepared to ruin our efforts and derail our aspirations. It is present when we look in the mirror, with our friends, and with our family. Our thoughts, feelings, and every cell in our bodies are all affected by anxiety. It causes headaches, allergies, tense muscles, frazzled nerves, unsettled stomachs, and sweaty palms. Every time we bite our nails, check the front door twice, decline an invitation, or engage in any other taught action, it is there.

I'm trying to explain that I'm not sure what anxiety looks like for you specifically. I might discuss regret, rumination, low self-esteem, unhealthy habits, and dysfunctional thought patterns. You may be able to relate to some of these and not others. The worry tree has many branches, but as you read, I hope you can see where its roots are in your particular circumstance. I want to share all I've discovered with you in this book, including all the tactics, methods, and suggestions I've discovered to help you develop self-compassion, improve your thought processes, and look after your physical and mental well-being.

Chapter 1

Humans and Anxiety

Of all emotions, fear is arguably the most fundamental. In addition to everyone experiencing it, fear responses have been discovered in every kind of animal, even in sea slugs. The intensity of dread experiences varies greatly, ranging from mild uneasiness to intense horror and panic. The duration of the fear experience can also vary, from a quick, almost fleeting flash to a persistent, daylong feeling. While worry and panic are unpleasant by nature, they are not in the least way dangerous.

One word best describes the main purpose of the human alarm system: survival. To respond to threats to our life in the earliest days, humans needed a set of reactions that would activate. We will look more extensively at the intricacies of how the human alarm response functions later in this chapter. But let's consider the big picture for the time being. Assume you were tasked with creating the human alarm system with the main objective of assisting in human response to survival dangers. What would you do next? If you were wise, you would start by carefully analyzing the kinds of hazards that people were likely to encounter. Mother Nature created our warning system precisely this way. She understood that there were two types of dangers that our alarm system needed to be able to respond to.

In the early stages of our evolution, humans frequently encountered impending hazards, such as coming face to face with a predator or being attacked by an adversary, or tribe. Even if the types of immediate risks we face today have evolved, we occasionally still run across an instant threat or danger. The priority in these immediately dangerous circumstances is to flee if at all possible, or to fight if escape is not an option. Evolutionary scientists frequently refer to this alarm reaction as the "Fight or Flight Response."Today, we refer to this reaction as panic, however, regrettably, some also use the term panic attack.

Mother Nature, however, was clever enough to recognize that not all hazards or dangers that humans face are immediate. Also, we required a reliable alert response for future hazards like a distant storm or the potential threat of a predatory or aggressive tribe. Future hazards in the modern world can include the impending final exam, the upcoming quarterly performance review, or the abnormal medical test result. The fight or flight response (panic), which is not necessary and can even be counterproductive in the case of these risks, is not required because they do not present a direct threat. To better equip us to handle potential threats in the future, we instead needed a different kind of alert response. Anxiety is the second alarm response type. Anxiety serves as an alert for readiness. Consider it as the alarm that prompts us to organize our defenses in anticipation of a threat or danger in the future.

The types of threats that the panic and anxiety alarms are intended to help us with may differ, yet they still have a lot in common.

Consider them both as typical, inborn emotional reactions to the feeling of threat or danger. Simply put, this indicates that anxiety and panic attacks, like other emotional reactions, are a normal component of our human biology.

We do not need to learn how to blink or swallow, just as we do not need to learn how to become frightened or panicked. Instead, they are automatically activated in reaction to a perceived threat or danger. Take care of the adjective "normal" as well. Sadly, people who experience anxiety frequently think that panic or anxiety is negative, dangerous, or unnatural. Contrarily, without the assistance of anxiety and Nevertheless, if that had happened, humans would have vanished thousands of years ago.

In conclusion, the two components of the human alarm system are panic and anxiety. Panic is the typical protective alarm response to perceived immediate threats, whereas anxiety is the typical alarm response to perceived future threats. This is the main distinction between the two. For instance, while many of us may react anxiously to the prospect of losing our jobs (a future threat), all but the most experienced divers may experience fear if their oxygen supply is abruptly cut off while they are scuba diving at 100 feet (an immediate threat). Finally, Many people have a false impression that panic and anxiety are dangerous. On the other hand, when faced with urgent danger, fear is our natural protective reaction.

Human Alarm System Activation

The same fundamental activation mechanism causes both prongs of the human alarm response panic and anxiety to be activated. We stressed before that a feeling of threat is necessary for the human alarm system to activate. To demonstrate this idea, picture yourself unknowingly sitting comfortably in your chair while a psychotic individual is hiding behind you with a pistol pointing squarely at your head!

Which alarm reaction do you think you'll have?

This was a trap question, and if you responded with "anxiety" or "panic," you were the victim. As perception is necessary for the human alarm response to be activated, despite the actual danger, your alarm system would remain silent in this sad circumstance.

The process of perception is intricate. We continuously get information through one or more of our five senses: the sound of birds chirping, the taste of apple pie, the sight of children playing, the scent of freshly cut grass, or the touch of ocean wind. The sensory system, which is made up of sensory receptors, neural pathways, and particular brain regions, is a sophisticated and complicated component of the human central nervous system. Our perspective of the world around us is formed by our sensory system's primary job of bringing the physical world into our minds for analysis and interpretation.

The great majority of current sensory data is disregarded and does not go through additional processing. But processing information that is personally relevant comes naturally to us. Have you ever been conversing with someone at a big social event when all of a sudden, the sound of your name being mentioned draws your attention temporarily from across the room? How about the frequent occurrence of being caught in traffic and noticing that your eyes have been drawn to the sight of an automobile that is the same model as yours in the lane across from you? Both of these typical occurrences demonstrate the fundamental idea that processing information that is personally meaningful is a part of our biological makeup. Sensory information expressing a potential threat is processed first because of its critical survival importance.

Sensory data indicating a possible threat or hazard may originate inside of us or external to us (external source). The following are some examples of internal alarm triggers: our thoughts (such as, "She's going to leave me"), imagery (such as, "Imagine making a fool of yourself when giving a speech"), bodily reactions (such as, "Feel your heart race while climbing several flights of stairs"), and memories (recalling a close call with a vicious dog), Maybe even specific feelings like fear, guilt, or rage. The following are some examples of external alarm triggers: (a) information from other people (such as criticism); (b) specific situations; (c) particular things; (d) information from various media sources, such as books, songs, magazines, TV, or the internet.

An efficient alarm system must be able to trigger promptly to maximize our reaction to any potential risk. Threat perception, which is what drives the human alarm reaction, had to change as a result of this to become instantaneous. Thankfully, humans possess the ability to recognize a threat without a conscious threatening idea being present. Take the following instance into consideration to prove your point.

When you hear the screeching of brakes while talking to your neighbor while standing on the street, you turn to find a car coming straight toward you. The alarm response is triggered when the sensory information from the car's sight and sound is processed by the visual and auditory sensory systems in a split second. This allows you to quickly exit the vehicle in danger. Imagine the identical situation, but with an alarm system that didn't let you get out of the path until you consciously thought, "OMG, this car is about to strike me"! The apparent argument is that forcing us to consciously consider risks would hinder our capacity to react to them and, as a result, dramatically lower our chances of surviving. This explains why we see some alarm reactions as appearing "out of the blue."

Once triggered, three distinct systems that cooperate for anxiety and panic appear. The three systems are as follows: (a) the physical system, which consists of all physiological adjustments our bodies make to help us deal with perceived threats, such as an increase in heart rate, respiration, perspiration, and muscle tension; (b) the mental or cognitive system, which consists of our thoughts and perceptions; and (c) our sensory and motor systems.

problem-solving (worrying), a change in focus to the perceived threat and potential coping or safety measures; and (c) an action system with innate protective action tendencies. The three-alarm response systems have one thing in common: they are all designed to help us deal with the perceived threat. Also keep in mind that the brain, which serves as our body's central nervous system, controls the changes in each of these three systems. In laboratories around the world, researchers are painstakingly trying to understand the intricate brain mechanisms governing the emotions associated with fear, such as anxiety and panic. Although neuroscientists have made significant progress in understanding the neurocircuitry of the human alarm system.

Let's switch each of the three systems one at a time to get a more thorough explanation of what occurs in each system when our alarm system is triggered. Your fear of anxiety and panic may noticeably lessen as you gain knowledge about how our alarm system operates.

The Physical System Changes Related To Anxiety And Panic

Chemical Effects Of Panic

Many brain areas are active when a threat is felt. They include the periaqueductal gray region of the middle brain, which is in charge of setting up the body's defense mechanism, and the amygdala, the brain's fear center. The adrenal glands in the kidneys receive the order from the brain to release noradrenaline and adrenaline. These compounds serve as messengers for the sympathetic nervous system, which starts and maintains pre-activation. Our nervous system's parasympathetic branch "kicks in," stopping the release of these chemicals into the bloodstream once the perceived threat or danger has passed. Keep in mind that it takes time for the chemical messengers, such as adrenaline and noradrenaline, to be eliminated. Because of the chemicals that are still floating about in your body even after the threat has passed and your sympathetic nervous system has ceased responding, one is likely to feel tense or anxious for a while.

You must constantly tell yourself that this is harmless and completely normal. This is an adaptive function because danger has the propensity to reappear frequently, making it advantageous to be vigilant.

Cardiovascular Effects

The heart rate and the force of each heartbeat rise as a result of sympathetic nervous system activity. Each of these typical cardiac alterations has a crucial purpose, notably increasing the amount of oxygen delivered to the muscles required for fight-or-flight. The system for delivering oxygen is the heart.

The heart muscle can be compared to a squirt gun. Every time your heart beats, it's like pulling the trigger on a squirt gun. The quantity of water released rises when the trigger is pulled more frequently. Similarly to this, a higher heart rate improves blood flow to the major muscle groups. because more blood flow indicates that the muscles will receive more oxygen because blood transports oxygen.

Similarly to this, pressing the trigger of the squirt cannon harder results in more water being produced with each squirt. Each heartbeat's increased contraction force operates in the same manner. Stroke volume is the term used by cardiologists to describe the increased contraction force. Sometimes people misinterpret this normal variation in heart rate and power as a sign that their heart is malfunctioning, which further fuels their anxiety or even panic. Nothing is more false than it is. It's not surprising that the cardiac changes that take place during a human alarm reaction (panic or anxiety) are similar to those that take place during physical activity because our alarm system evolved to get us ready to run or fight.

The direction of the blood flow also changes, along with the heart's increasing activity. In essence, blood is diverted away from areas where it is not required (by a constriction of the blood vessels). For instance, blood is drawn away from the fingers, toes, and skin. This is advantageous because the organism is less likely to bleed to death if it is assaulted and cut in any way. As a result, when someone is anxious, their skin appears pale, feels cold, and their fingers and toes also become cold while occasionally becoming numb and tingly. Moreover, the blood is transferred to the arms and legs, which have muscles that require the most oxygen for flight or fighting.

Respiratory Effects

The alarm reaction is accompanied by an increase in breathing rate and/or depth. This is crucial for dealing with danger because running or fighting requires more oxygen for our muscles. Many of the threats we confront in today's world do not call for more oxygen to be present. As a result, when we are under stress, we frequently breathe in more oxygen than we require. For instance, breathing more oxygen is not necessary when you are sitting in a chair and fretting about a work presentation that is coming up.

When more oxygen is being consumed than is being used, it is said to be hyperventilating. It causes a cascade of physiological changes, including a decrease in blood CO_2 levels and an increase in blood pH, even though it is not hazardous in any manner. Lightheadedness, numbness or tingling in the hands, feet, or lips, sweating, an accelerated heart rate, thoughts of disbelief or spaciness, and tightness in the chest are just a few of the unpleasant (but innocuous) sensations brought on by these physiological changes. It's crucial to understand that hyperventilation can operate as a cause or catalyst for anxiety or panic as well as a response to stress, worry, panic, or other negative emotional states. Many people unknowingly experience hyperventilation. Excessive yawning, excessive breath holding, or feelings of breathlessness the subjective perception that one is not getting enough air are a few symptoms of chronic hyperventilation.

The good news is that hyperventilation can be readily controlled by taking moderate, shallow breaths through the nose or by engaging in aerobic exercise like running in place or climbing stairs.

Additional Physical Effects

Sweating increases when the alarm reaction is activated. Important adaptive functions include cooling the body to prevent overheating and making the skin more slippery to make it difficult for a predator to grab.

The sympathetic nervous system's activation causes several additional effects, none of which are in any way dangerous. For instance, when the pupils dilate to let in more light, this can cause vision blur, spots in front of the eyes, etc.

Saliva production is reduced, which results in having a dry mouth. Digestion is less active, which frequently results in nausea, a heavy feeling in the stomach, and even constipation. Finally, in preparation for fight or flight, several muscle groups stiffen up, which causes subjective feelings of tension that can occasionally include physical pain as well as trembling and shaking. That is typical since the human alarm response demands a lot of energy.

Changes In The Mental System Related To Anxiety And Panic

The purpose of the human alarm system, as was previously emphasized, is to aid the individual in responding to impending hazards. Mother Nature programmed the Alert system to focus our attention on the possible threat and divert our attention from present tasks to achieve that goal. This alert feature helps us when there are genuine risks that require our attention, but it causes us significant problems when the perceived threats are false, like in the example of the father who can't hear the alarm.

His laser-beam focus on the harmless sensations of lightheadedness that he has misinterpreted as an indication of a brain tumor prevents him from even focusing on a conversation with his child.

Worry is another mental component of the anxiety alert. One way to think of worry is as mental problem-solving. We have been given the ability to create what-if scenarios, generate potential solutions to issues, and weigh the likely effects of those solutions. Compared to lower-order species that lack problem-solving skills, worry offers a significant evolutionary advantage in fending off potential threats. The mental problem-solving that takes place when there is no actual issue to solve, however, can cause worry to become pathological and result in anxiety disorders. In this situation, worry serves no adaptive purpose and instead gets in the way of our ability to concentrate on leading a fulfilling life.

Changes In The Action System Related To Panic And Anxiety

Not to mention, there are essential behaviors that have been ingrained in us by evolution to achieve the fundamental objective of survival. In contrast to our lower-order animal relatives, who respond to certain situations with very specific fixed behaviors (such as deer initially freezing to a car beam), we, on the other hand, have a wide range of flexible behaviors.

Evolutionary biologists refer to these inclinations as emotional action tendencies, and we humans have them because of our more complex brains. Action tendency is a term that is frequently used incorrectly. The word "tendency" is used here to underline how, even if certain behaviors or actions are linked to each emotion, we can suppress these reactions when they are not necessary. Consider the scenario of seeing a fast train coming your way in a 3-D movie theater. Most of us don't run from the theater in a fit of panic. Why? With cognitive reframing of the event as a "simply a scenario," we can suppress the primal terror response.

you are not actually about to get splattered all over the theater by a train as you watch a "movie".

When treating people with anxiety disorders, the ability to control or overcome action patterns becomes extremely important.

When a panic or anxiety alarm is triggered, the major classes of action tendencies are different. Panic is characterized in large part by the need to run, escape, or perhaps even fight (perceived immediate threat). We frequently encounter circumstances in daily life that we want to flee from or avoid. The fight-or-flight reaction, as previously mentioned, primes the body for movement either to attack or to flee. It follows that it is not surprising that the overwhelming need to flee is connected to the panic alert. When societal restrictions prevent this, the desires are frequently expressed through actions like pacing, foot tapping, or snapping at other people. Overall, sensations of being entrapped and the desire to flee are developed.

Chapter 2

Thought is not the Enemy

We all reside in an extremely intellectual, overstimulated, and high-strung world.

Our natural cognitive processes go into overdrive when we overthink something.

When our brain processes spiral out of control and cause us tension, it is called excessive thinking. Continuous self- and life-analysis are typically undesirable, unavoidable, and harmful. Normally, our brains aid in problem-solving and better understanding, but excessive pondering has the opposite effect.

Whatever you want to call it worry, anxiety, stress, rumination, or even obsession overthinking always has one thing in common: it feels terrible and does us no good. Typical overthinking makes thoughts seem obtrusive and frequently magnifies themselves or runs in loops indefinitely.

Whether the mental activity includes analyzing, judging, monitoring, evaluating, controlling, worrying or all of them, overthinking is an overly damaging mental activity. If the following applies to you, overthinking may be a problem:

You frequently are aware of your thoughts as they are happening.

You think about your thoughts or participate in metacognition.

You make an effort to manage or direct your ideas.

You find it upsetting or unpleasant to have unplanned ideas, and you frequently believe that some thoughts are unwanted.

For you, thinking frequently resembles a fight between opposing urges.

You often dispute, examine, or critique your thoughts. You frequently blame yourself and your thoughts for the issue.

You are concentrating on comprehending your thoughts and exploring the workings of your mind.

There are many things you worry about and are concerned about. You have trouble making decisions and frequently second-guess the ones you do make. You notice that you repeatedly engage in negative thought patterns.

Sometimes, even if a notion is in the past and nothing can be done about it, you feel as though you can't help thinking about it repeatedly.

You'll see that some of the aforementioned traits are debatably positive ones. Don't we all want to develop our awareness and mindfulness? Isn't it wise to reflect on your automatic responses and pose difficult questions to yourself to make more informed choices? Overthinking, as its name suggests, is when we think beyond what is in our best interests. Thinking is a wonderful talent. The most distinguishing trait of humanity and the reason for many of our triumphs is undoubtedly our capacity for reflection, analysis, and even self-examination. No one is against thought. Our brain is a remarkably useful instrument, yet when we overthink, we simply reduce its effectiveness.

Causes of Mental Chaos and Anxiety

Why does overthinking happen so frequently and so easily if the brain is such a lovely thing and thinking is so beneficial? Individuals have put forth theories throughout history (presumably overthinkers): perhaps overthinking is a negative habit, a personality trait, or a mental condition that can be treated with medication. Persons who overthink frequently develop a preoccupation with the causes of their overthinking. "Why am I acting this way? "

If you've chosen to read this book, it's likely that you've felt frustrated by how easily your mind may wander. But, there are remedies and a path out of the chaos and tension and into the calmer, clearer seas. Perhaps the most important thing to remember is that overthinking rarely focuses on its causes.

The troubles may be the thoughts while we are mired in rumination.

When anything bothers us, we convince ourselves, "If I could only get rid of it, I could relax and everything would be OK." But, even if that issue were to be remedied, another one would inevitably replace it. This is so because it was always the outcome of overthinking rather than the cause. Instead of attempting to solve the issue from within our own rumination, we must take a step back if we are to successfully combat overthinking. For the remainder of this book, we'll proceed under the premise that anxiousness is what we're referring to when we talk about overthinking. Even without a formal diagnosis of an anxiety disorder, people can overthink. But in the subsequent chapters, we'll discover that anxiousness is the underlying factor (the why), and overthinking is the result (the how). So where does anxiousness originate from?

Where does worry originate?

The origins of anxiety disorders are not fully understood since there is no single factor that creates anxiety; rather, a number of elements, both physical and psychological, interact to produce it. Heredity likely plays a part in the prevalence of anxiety disorders in some families. On a psychological level, anxiety is seen as a reaction to environmental pressures, such as the end of a meaningful relationship or exposure to a tragedy that poses a serious threat to life.

An anxiety disorder can develop when a person reacts inappropriately to stress or when they feel overtaken by events. For instance, some people find it thrilling to speak in front of a group. Others, however, dread it and experience symptoms of anxiety including perspiration, panic, a quick heartbeat, and occasionally even tremors.

Even in a small gathering, such individuals may refrain from speaking. A physical condition or the usage of a drug are two additional possible causes of anxiety disorders. For instance, anxiety can be brought on by an overactive thyroid, adrenal gland, or tumor called a pheochromocytoma. Corticosteroids, cocaine, amphetamines, ephedrine, and sometimes too much caffeine are among the drugs that might make you anxious.

Alcohol or certain sedative withdrawal might also result in anxiety disorder symptoms. Dementia may be the most frequent source of worry among elderly adults. However, the precise reason for various anxiety disorders is not yet fully known.

There are numerous varieties of worry as well as numerous ways in which it can manifest. Two categories are frequently used to categorize anxiety-related causes:

Environmental

Biological

The experiences that can generate anxiety are referred to as "environmental" causes of anxiety. They might be the environment you grew up in, any stresses you're going through right now, or a tragic experience you had.

All factors that can be linked to your Genes and/or current physical health are considered "biological" causes of anxiety. In addition to heredity, physical changes to the brain, health problems, and drug use can all be examples of potential biological factors that contribute to anxiety.

Let's start with a typical justification for anxiousness.

Is anxiety inherited?

Your parents have a big influence on a lot of who you are. Your physical features, talents, and even some aspects of your personality are genetically inherited from one generation to the next. This frequently prompts individuals to question whether anxiety disorders might also be passed down from parents.

The biochemistry of anxiety is still being studied, and we still don't fully understand it. Yet, researchers have found a link between a person's risk of developing an anxiety illness and specific genes.

Scientists are examining how anxiety might be transmitted from a parent to a child as part of their research on "inherited anxiety." Genes, or the components of your genetic composition, are the main mechanism by which this occurs. Each gene includes all the data necessary to determine traits like your writing hand and hair color, as well as details about how your body and brain work.

Both of your parents pass on their DNA to you. Your father gave you the other pair, while your mother gave you the first. Some of the genes your parents contain will not be passed down to you, whilst other genes will be carried even if your parents don't exhibit the features.

According to research, some genes increase a person's risk of developing phobias, social anxiety, panic disorder, obsessive-compulsive disorder, and generalized anxiety. Certain genetic traits may be passed down from parent to child, making siblings frequently share them.

One or more of these genes may run in your family if you have a history of anxiety or have close relatives who suffer from the condition. You might be at a higher risk of acquiring anxiety as a result of this.

The problem is that there is no evidence that these genes in particular induce anxiety. Instead, they seem to be just another component at play. While it is true that heredity can contribute to any anxiety disorders you may have over the course of your life, this is by no means the only factor. Whether not or anxiety runs in your family, there are many causes for anxiety, and understanding the role genetics play can help you better understand your risks and the underlying causes of any anxiety you experience.

Is our environment a cause of anxiety?

Your incredibly fair skin may burn in the sun more than other people's skin due to your genes, but the sun determines whether you burn or not. Similar to how genes predispose us in one direction or another, life itself has the most impact on how anxiety is developed and maintained. In other words, overthinking is a result of both genetic tendencies and stressful triggering events.

The conventional wisdom used to think that mental problems were solely caused by "chemical imbalances" in the brain of the individual who had them.

But as we now know, living in a highly stressful environment may undoubtedly lead to anxiety and other mental health issues. Stress is beneficial. The type of regular, everyday pressure that motivates us, keeps us alert and pushes us to improve is referred to as "eustress" or positive stress. Nevertheless, excessive stress has the opposite impact and merely serves to drain our psychological reserves, leaving us feeling helpless to cope. On the other hand, a complete absence of stimulation can also make us agitated. This type of stress, known as hypostasis, happens when our environment isn't challenging us enough. This merely serves to demonstrate that to thrive, we require an environment that is best suited to our requirements rather than one that is stress-free. Anxiety and stress are distinct emotions.

Anxiety is our internal perception of this pressure, whereas stress is something external to us that we experience. Because everyone has different inner resources and thresholds, we all react to stressful situations in different ways. These reactions can include additional emotions (like anger or depression) as well as physical symptoms (like insomnia, digestive trouble, or lack of concentration).

Life itself is difficult. To feel pressurized, challenged, or uncomfortable is commonplace in our everyday lives. But if it persists and exceeds our capacity for survival, we risk becoming worn out, depressed, or suffering from an anxiety illness. The fight-or-flight reaction in the body developed to keep us safe, but we were never meant to maintain a constant state of hyperarousal. It is a recipe for burnout and overwhelming to add prolonged stress to someone who already has a biological or psychological propensity to overthinking.

Work pressures, demanding kids, a stifling relationship, the constant stress of the 24-hour news cycle, politics, climate change, your noisy upstairs neighbor, a lack of sleep, eating too much junk food, that terrible event from last year, your low money balance... It's not surprising that a lot of us feel totally overwhelmed. Last but not least, our own conduct and attitudes have a significant role in influencing our propensity to acquire anxiety disorders.

Are our mental models the cause of our anxiety?

The narrative we tell about our lives, the way we interpret events, our internal dialogue, and our sense of who we are as people all fall at the intersection of nature and nurture. It's not the load, but how you bear it, goes the proverb. Depending on how you see and comprehend an event, as well as how you actively interact with it, or what decisions you make, will determine whether you perceive it as stressful or overwhelming. The same scenario can be interpreted very differently by two people; it is the interpretation, not the scenario, that determines how they feel. Some assessments of life merely produce more stressful results. If you're the type of person who, for instance, believes that luck, chance, or other people have more control over your life than you have, you might perceive a certain new scenario as a threat rather than an exhilarating challenge. And after convincing yourself that it poses a threat, you will act accordingly and become anxious.

Your interpretation of neutral occurrences depends on your views, viewpoints, sense of self, worldview, and cognitive models.

We react to our sense of stress rather than actual stress. You won't find suggestions on how to alter your genetic makeup (impossible) or reduce environmental stress (slightly more doable, but still not by much) in the pages that follow. Instead, we'll concentrate on all the things you have the power to do right now to alter your perspective and more effectively control worry and overthinking.

Those who overthink frequently attribute their behavior to hereditary and environmental factors, but ultimately it is their particular evaluation that ties everything together in a uniquely stressful way. What do you think about your natural propensities for stress resistance? What do you think about them? How do you see the challenges in the world, and how much control do you have over how things turn out? What routines do you follow each day? Do you feel happy about yourself? How do your boundaries stand up? All of these are within our power to alter.

Consequences of Anxiety

Long-term and short-term physical consequences can include a racing heart, headache, nausea, muscle tension, exhaustion, dry mouth, dizziness, increase in breathing rate, aching muscles, trembling and twitching, sweating, disordered digestion, immune system suppression, and memory problems. Your body was built to withstand brief bursts of acute stress, but continuing stress can start to lead to chronic health concerns including heart disease, sleeplessness, hormonal dysregulation, and other things. The physical impacts of stress can have an impact on your lifelong health if they persist for a long time.

Examples of mental and psychological effects include weariness, feeling on edge, anxiety, irritability, lack of focus, lack of motivation, changes in libido and appetite, nightmares, depression, feeling out of control, apathy, and other symptoms. Stress can erode our motivation, diminish our confidence, and reinforce damaging self-talk behaviors.

Disruption of intimate relationships, poor performance at work, anger, impatience with others, withdrawing socially, and engaging in addictive or destructive behaviors are some of the most significant social and environmental impacts. A person who is nervous and stressed out all the time tends to lose all sense of purpose in life, quits making plans, is unable to act with kindness or compassion toward others, and loses enthusiasm for living.

As you might expect, the interaction between the physical, mental, and environmental factors results in a single, cohesive experience of worry and overthinking.

For instance, if you continually overthink, your body will produce large amounts of cortisol and other stress hormones. This can make you feel on edge and even make you overthink more, which increases stress and alters how you feel about yourself and your life. The stress cycle you're in may be furthered if you choose unwisely for yourself (e.g., staying up late, eating terrible food, or cutting people off). You might work less effectively, put off tasks, give yourself more to worry about, and so on.

Chapter 3

Organize your thoughts

Four Factors That Create Mental Clutter

Understanding why you have these thoughts is crucial before beginning any of the techniques to stop your negative thinking.

We'll discuss four of these reasons for mental clutter in this section.

Reason #1: Daily stress

The main cause of why so many people experience life-overwhelm is excessive stress. The stress brought on by physical clutter, an abundance of information, and the unending choices these items demand can lead to a variety of mental health problems like melancholy, panic attacks, and generalized anxiety. Our psyches look for exits when life gets too demanding and confusing. A less-than-healthy coping reaction can be brought on by excessive input, unfavorable exposure, and choices.

Reason #2: The Choice Dilemma

In terms of mental health, the freedom of choice, which is prized in free societies, might have a declining point of return. The term "paradox of choice," which was coined by psychologist Barry Schwartz, sums up his research showing that having more options causes people to feel more anxious, uncertain, paralyzed, and unsatisfied. Although having more options may result in objectively superior outcomes, you won't be delighted with them.

Reason #3: Having too much "stuff"

Clothes we never wear, books we won't read, unplayed with toys, and underutilized technology are all over our homes. Our inboxes on computers are full. Messages like "You need more storage" are flashing on our phones and our PCs, respectively. Because we've become such gadget slaves, we prefer instant entertainment or information to interactions and experiences in the actual world. Having access to technology and the constant flow of information makes it simpler than ever to become a mass consumer of goods and information. We can order anything online and have it delivered to our home, from a book to a motorboat, with the press of a button. We are overstuffing our homes with unnecessary items and spending all of our free time reading tweets, updates, articles, blog posts, and cat videos.

Around us, information and things are accumulating, but we feel powerless to do something about it. We can't give up everything we have in this world and live in a cave. We need to find a means to survive in the present day without going insane.

Some of the tension and negative thoughts might be relieved by organizing our belongings and spending less time on technology. But there are still many reasons for us to get bogged down in regret, worry, and other negative thoughts.

We fret about a variety of things, including terrorism, politics, pain from the past, our uncertain futures, and our health, jobs, kids, relationships, economics, and appearance.

Our time and productivity are both wasted by all of this unnecessary information, which also causes reactive, nervous, and pessimistic thinking.

Like: " It seems as though my Facebook friend is enjoying life. My life is terrible.

Should I purchase Fitbit and begin monitoring my health so I don't pass away too soon?

Oh crap, I completely forgot about that webinar on "How to Earn a Million Before You're 30"what if they revealed something crucial?

Everything appears urgent and vital. Responses to all emails and texts are required. Every new gadget or contraption needs to be bought. This keeps us distracted from the people around us and the emotions inside of us, continuously riled up, and preoccupied with unimportant things.

We frequently believe that we are too busy ingesting new things and information to have time to simplify. Yet eventually, all of this activity is wearing us out mentally and emotionally. We scrutinize, ruminate, and stress ourselves to the breaking point as we try to process all that is being presented to us.

How did we come to forget the principles and goals in life that used to keep us centered and sane? How can we handle it? We are unable to travel back in time and abandon technology. We cannot completely relinquish everything. If we didn't have that constant voice in our heads stirring things up, we wouldn't suffer from our thoughts about these things and would be happier right now.

Reason #4: The negativity bias

Although the neurological system of humans has evolved over 600 million years, it still reacts in the same way as it did for our distant ancestors who confronted danger every day and only needed it to survive.

But what does your thinking have to do with the negative bias? It implies that you have a biological tendency to overanalyze events, worry excessively, and see the worst possible side of everything. You perceive challenges as more challenging and threats as more dangerous Any unfavorable notion that enters your head feels real, and you tend to take it as gospel. But, you do not always face danger because you do not live in a cave. You don't have to accept your tendency to think negatively just because it's part of your genetic makeup.

Just associating with the first notion that enters consciousness is not the only option. This substitute is mindfulness. The most routine tasks can be used to develop mindfulness, and it can be fostered through the specific exercises offered throughout this book.

Retraining your brain to remain out of the mental clutter from the future and concentrate on the present now is required for mindfulness. You stop attaching to your thoughts when you are mindful. Simply said, you are present in whatever it is that you are doing.

Seems easy, doesn't it? Though the idea seems straightforward, it might be challenging to alter your way of thinking.

Decluttering your mind involves practice, persistence, and the ability to start small before expanding from there, just like developing any other habit.

Thankfully, we'll demonstrate how to accomplish each of these throughout this book.

Along with learning how to regulate your thoughts and train your brain, you'll also develop the everyday habits that will support these mental exercises.

We'll discuss four practices you can adopt to clear your mind of clutter in the remaining paragraphs of this section. As you get more adept at thinking, you'll discover that you'll become more productive and focused as well as more at ease with the absurd demands of contemporary life.

Now let's get started with the first routine that will teach your brain to breathe focused.

Habit #1 of Mental Decluttering: Concentrated Deep Breathing

You probably don't think about your breathing very much, despite the fact that you take roughly 20,000 breaths every day. Your brain automatically modifies your breathing to meet your body's needs. You don't have to think, "I should breathe deeper and harder to deliver more oxygen to my muscles," when running or climbing stairs. It simply occurs. It is the responsibility of sensors in your brain, blood vessels, muscles, and lungs to adjust your breathing to your body's changing needs. Nonetheless, you have the authority to do so whenever you desire. Breathing can be slowed down, changed from the chest to the abdomen, and even made shallower or deeper.

The first indication that our thoughts are intense and overwhelming is frequently a change in respiration. We may breathe quickly or get short of breath when we are stressed, unhappy, harried, or upset. Poor, shallow breathing is also a result of our contemporary lifestyles and work environments. Sadly, we spend much of the day sitting still, so we don't need to breathe deeply like our ancestors did while they were out hunting, gathering, farming, or doing other hard labor. We have gotten into the habit of short, shallow breathing whether we are slouched over our workstations or watching TV on the couch.

When we're hurried and pressed for time, we breathe quickly and nervously. Our bodies constrict when we're under stress, apprehensive, or preoccupied with a problem, and we hunch forward with our heads bowed, arms clasped, and muscles taut.

These positions all restrict respiration. Sometimes, the muscles that move the thorax, regulate inhalation, and cause muscular tension clamp down like a vice to limit exhalation, causing us to completely forget to breathe. You might not give your breathing or posture much thought, but by merely paying attention to your breathing, you can promote a calmer state of body and mind.

Simply start focusing on your breathing to become more conscious of how you are breathing throughout the day.

While developing the focused deep breathing habit, we advise remembering the following four things:

1. Sit up straighter to give your lungs more room to take in oxygen rather than slouching at your desk or on the couch at home.

Become conscious of any tight spots in your body, and then mentally "breathe into" those spots, imagining them loosening up as you do.

2. Always breathe through your nose as opposed to your mouth. Impurities and air that is too chilly are kept out of your body by defense mechanisms in your nose. Poisonous gases that could injure you can also be detected by your nose.

Let your nose do the breathing; mouth breathing can allow bacteria and viruses into your lungs.

3. To breathe through as if you were filling your stomach, use abdominal breathing by gently pushing your stomach outward. Slowly exhale while allowing your tummy to settle back into its regular position.

4. Recognize the difference between abdominal or diaphragmatic breathing, which fills the lower lobes of the lungs and promotes complete oxygen exchange, and shallow breathing, which stops at the chest. With the movements of the diaphragm, abdominal breathing also massages the abdominal organs.

Breathing slowly, deeply, and rhythmically is one of the finest ways to distance yourself from unfavorable thoughts and regain control over your thoughts. By encouraging the parasympathetic nervous system, this concentrated breathing lowers heart rate, relaxes muscles, calms the mind, and restores normal brain function.

Your body will feel more attuned to you as a result of deep breathing, which will also help you stop worrying and calm your mind's internal dialogue.

The "relaxation response" is the term used to describe the physiological modifications brought on by deep breathing. The benefits of deep nose breathing are as follows:

increase the production of nitric oxide, a potent immune-stimulating chemical made in the sinuses during nasal breathing. Remove impurities from your body and enhance oxygenation to your blood to improve its quality. through a stomach and digestive system that is more effective, and aids in the absorption and assimilation of food. By increasing oxygenation, you can improve the nervous system's condition and performance.

Increased circulation will help the heart and stomach organs perform better.

As the lungs grow stronger, this will aid in preventing respiratory issues. The heart becomes stronger and more effective, and the workload on the heart is decreased, which lowers blood pressure and helps avoid heart disease.

help you lose weight because greater oxygen helps you burn fat more effectively.

You can create a lifelong habit that has been shown through years of research and testing to help you calm your mind and body by engaging in daily deep abdominal breathing for a few minutes. Anywhere, at any time, is a good place to practice mindful breathing, but it works best when you're overthinking or feeling pressured and nervous. Your sense of well-being and mental tranquility can be enhanced by engaging in even brief periods of mindful breathing each day.

But, since concentrated breathing is the cornerstone of a meditation practice, which we'll cover in the following chapter, you might wish to establish a regular practice of deep breathing at a particular time of day. You may simply use this habit as a trigger and beginning point for your meditation practice if you develop a 5- to 10-minute breathing routine.

You can utilize the following seven steps to establish the everyday practice of deep breathing:

1. Pick a time of day to practice deep breathing; ideally, it should come right after a daily ritual you follow religiously, like brushing your teeth. Since it sets the tone for your day, practicing in the morning is always a smart idea. As your

workday progresses, though, you could discover that you need to take a break in the middle of it. Another wonderful time is right before bed because it encourages a peaceful condition right before sleep.

2. Decide on a location for your breathing exercise that is quiet and free of distractions or interruptions. Disconnect from your computer, phone, and any other devices that can annoy you.

3. Set a 10-minute timer.

4. Sit in a meditative position, such as the lotus position, on the floor with a pillow, or a chair with your feet flat on the ground. Lay your hands down in your lap softly.

5. Allow your stomach to expand as you slowly inhale through your nose until your lungs are fully inflated.

6. Hold your breath for two counts as you exhale.

7. Let your breath out completely and slowly, allowing your stomach to reposition itself. There should also be a pause after each breath.

Don't breathe in too much air at once when you initially start.

Start by inhaling for four counts, pausing for two counts, and then exhaling for four counts. Reduce your inhalation depth if you start to hyperventilate. Your lung capacity will increase with practice, allowing you to breathe in more air.

Let's move on to another mindfulness exercise that also involves concentrated breathing but elevates your degree of peace, tranquility, and calmness.

Habit #2 of mental decluttering: Meditation

To meditate, you don't need to be a Buddhist, mystic, or ex-hippie holding a crystal. Anybody can benefit from meditation and use it as a tool to clear their mind, regardless of their spiritual or religious affiliation or lack thereof. The thought of sitting still in the lotus position and emptying your mind may be off-putting if you've never meditated or are unfamiliar with it. But don't let the cliches about cave dwellers who practice meditation stop you from trying it.

Since it has been around for so long, meditation has its roots in the ancient Buddhist, Hindu, and Chinese traditions. There are many different types of meditation, but they all start with the same steps: sitting still, concentrating on your breath, and ignoring any outside distractions. Depending on the method of meditation practiced and the desired results of the practitioner, many goals can be set for meditation. For the purposes of this article, we recommend meditation as a tool to assist you in developing mental discipline and thought control, both while you are sitting in meditation and when you are not.

The advantages of meditation carry over to your daily life, assisting you in reducing anxiety and overthinking as well as offering a variety of health advantages, which we'll go over below.

Just practicing meditation can help you become successful at it. You can develop your meditation techniques and learn how the mental, physical, and emotional advantages get better with practice. Although the process of meditation is easy to follow, it is not as simple as it first appears.

You'll learn that initially trying to quiet your mind and stay focused is like trying to train fleas. However, the experience gets simpler and more fun the more you practice.

Here is a quick 11-step procedure you can apply to develop the habit of meditation:

1. Choose a calm, serene area where you can close the door to be completely alone for your meditation practice.

2. Select a particular hour of the day for your practice. You can use this as your trigger (and beginning point) for your new meditation habit if you've started a deep breathing routine. Alternatively, you can select a different trigger and meditate at a different time of day.

3. Choose whether you want to meditate while seated in a straight-back chair or sofa or on a pillow on the floor. Avoid reclining while meditating since you might nod off.

4. Eliminate all sources of distraction and switch off any digital or other noisy equipment. Eliminate pets from the space.

5. Set a 10-minute timer.

6. Take a seat comfortably, either in a chair or in a cushioned cross-legged position on the floor. Keep your hands lightly in your lap and your spine straight.

7. Close your eyes or keep them open while focusing your gaze downward, and then take three to four slow, deep breaths through your nose.

8. Gradually start to pay attention to your breathing. While you breathe in and out, pay attention to how your chest and abdomen rise and fall. Do not force your breaths; instead, let them occur naturally.

9. Pay close attention to how you are breathing; you might even mentally think the words "in" and "out" as you inhale and exhale, respectively.

10. In the beginning, your thoughts will stray frequently. As they do, gently let them go before turning your focus back to your breathing.

Keep in mind that having intrusive thoughts is normal. Your "monkey mind" is simply trying to take over at that point. Bring your attention back to your breathing and keep it there.

Initially, you might need to repeat this a dozen times.

11. You'll probably become aware of other perceptions and sensations as you concentrate on breathing, such as sounds, physical discomfort, emotions, etc.

Simply take note of them as they enter your awareness, and then slowly come back to your breathing feeling.

Your aim is to gradually turn into a witness to every sound, sensation, feeling, and thought as it appears and vanishes. Look at them as if you were watching them from a distance, without judging or making any internal remarks.

You eventually get more and more control of your mind and your capacity to refocus it on the present rather than letting it take over and flee anytime a notion or distraction appears. You'll initially feel as though your monkey mind is constantly at war with you. Yet, with time and practice, you won't need to constantly change your focus. Your mind automatically starts to open up to the great calm and vastness of simply being here as thoughts start to gradually fade away. This is a tranquil and fulfilling experience.

The silent interval between ideas is referred to by meditation teachers as the "gap" or state of calm. The gap is initially relatively small, and it is challenging to stay there for more than a few nanoseconds. The gap will widen and open more frequently as you practice meditation, allowing you to relax there for longer amounts of time. Try the following exercise to experience a fleeting instant of the pause between thoughts: Eyes closed, start to become aware of your thoughts.

Just pause for a moment and watch them arrive and go. Then, consider where your subsequent thought will originate. As you wait for the response, pause. When you wait for the response, you could notice that there is a brief pause in your thinking. You can also put yourself in a deep listening mode to practice this "space between thoughts" exercise. Try to hear a soft, faraway sound by remaining still while paying close attention. Once more, you are awake, alert, and waiting without being diverted by thought. At the beginning of your meditation practice, you might not experience a gap moment. You might discover that you are continuously changing the subject of your thoughts, paying attention to your physical discomforts, and questioning why you are even bothering with this pointless activity.

You could be hard on yourself for not "doing it right" or doubt whether you are improving at all. Your thoughts may veer off into a meandering conversation about how you're feeling and how the meditation is going while you're trying to focus. Or, if you have a minute of space between thoughts, you can become preoccupied with the excitement of finally having it.

It is always your responsibility to observe and bring your attention back to the present, to your breathing.

Your meditation practice is not intended to help you achieve nirvana or a spiritual epiphany. Simply put, you're trying to exert more mental restraint until your mind gets the message and caves. Your efforts will lead to a mental home that you manage, not one that is managed by you.

Habit # 3 of mental decluttering: Reframe all negative thoughts

Our ability to think critically is essential to our survival and ability to compete in the modern world. We are able to rapidly and efficiently address difficulties thanks to critical thinking. Our ability to think creatively enables us to create unique, varied, and complex relationships.

But, it is an unwelcome negative thought that clogs our minds and frequently saps our zest for life. Many people experience victimization of their bad beliefs throughout their entire lives. They believe the "voices" in their heads that warn them the sky is falling because they believe they have no control over the thoughts that live in their brains.

Even while the negative bias exists, you can still change it and become more self-aware by making an effort. Though it might seem normal to let your thoughts drift into worry and despair, by choosing not to challenge them and accepting your thoughts as who you are, you have reinforced negative thinking. Nevertheless, by developing the reframing habit, you have the ability to notice this inclination and change it.

Recognizing your thought patterns and stopping them before they spiral out of hand is the first step. Here are six techniques you can employ throughout the day to alter the pattern and start controlling your thoughts.

Using each of these techniques only takes a few minutes.

Rule #1: Act as a Watcher

Become conscious of your ideas first. Distinguish your "self" from your thoughts, then pay attention to what's happening in your head.

The difficulty is to approach this objectively, without passing judgment on any one thought. Just be aware of yourself as an impartial observer of your ideas.

This practice can be performed intermittently during the day or while meditating. Your thoughts and the feelings they engender lose their potency when you choose to observe them rather than identify with them.

Rule #2: Identify That Idea

By recognizing in your mind that your thoughts are just that—thoughts—and not your reality, you can further distance yourself from them.

For instance, instead of saying, "I'll never get all of this done," say, "I'm having the thought that I'll never get all of this done."

This serves as further evidence that you are not your ideas.

Rule #3: Simply say no

Simply exclaim, "STOP!" out loud (vocalizing encourages the interruption), and then picture a thick metal wall crashing down in front of your wandering thoughts whenever you discover yourself in a mental loop or feeling anxious.

Sometimes, You can imagine shoving bad thoughts down a rabbit hole or into a balloon that floats away.

Rule #4: use the rubber band trick

wristband made of rubber is recommended. Every time you see it, pause and become aware of your thoughts. Put the rubber band on the opposite wrist or gently pop it on your wrist if you find yourself thinking only negatively. This bodily activity halts the progression of unfavorable thoughts.

Rule #5: Recognize Your Triggers

Overthinking and pessimism are frequently brought on by someone, something, or something bodily. Take attention to the regular concerns and apprehensions you dwell on.

Do these triggers ever occur in your mind for any reason?

If so, make a list of the triggers so you can keep track of when they occur. Being aware of it can help you avoid being surprised by unfavorable thoughts.

Rule #6: divert your attention

Use diversion to break the pattern. Engage in mental activity to keep your mind from wandering to unpleasant ideas. Become lost in a task that requires concentration and mental effort.

Try to memorize a poem or run through your multiplication tables in your head if you're stopped in traffic or standing in line.

Habit #4 of Mental Decluttering: Learn New Mind Tricks

Being more proactive with what you let stay in your thoughts will help you control the discomfort, though.

The process of retraining your brain and learning to dissociate from bad thoughts involves more than just interrupting cluttered thinking. You must fill the space with useful thoughts since your mind hates a vacuum to avoid reverting to previous habits.

The following four options are available to you:

#1. Reject the Thought and Replace It

You could find that a lot of your thoughts are absurdly exaggerated. These aren't the truth, or at least not the whole truth. You may believe, "I'm a loser, I can never do anything well." You may feel defeated at the time, but upon closer inspection, you realize that the feeling is not totally accurate. You've accomplished a lot of things and have been prosperous frequently.

Challenge any "all or nothing" thoughts you might have. This just entails thinking of a specific instance that disproves the idea by reminding oneself of a happy occasion or prior "victory."

Let's take the scenario where you are a writer and a recent book gets a bad review. At first, you could believe, "I'm a terrible writer everyone hates what I write." the bulk of your readers, however, clearly adore your content if you take the time to read the 100 prior good evaluations.

Though it may feel strange at first, you'll gradually develop the ability to break those negative thought patterns. With the aid of this habit, you may take charge of your reality and put a stop to the never-ending motorway of self-defeating ideas.

#2 Practice Acceptance

What you do about those negative thoughts that are true is one question that you can have. Or, how do you handle situations where there is a good cause to think negatively?

The fact is that there will be times when you'll feel like it's difficult to keep a happy attitude. It's also true, though, that our perceptions of these difficult circumstances are frequently much worse than the actual circumstances.

During difficult circumstances, you cannot totally banish your unhappy thoughts, but you can diminish them via acceptance. Your mental pain increases when you fight against the reality of a difficult situation. You can't force a solution on yourself by worry or shame. You need a peaceful mind and a clear head instead.

Stop for a moment and just say, "I accept this scenario is happening," whenever you catch yourself straining and ruminating. Take a deep breath and try not to battle it in your head any longer. You can... as you start to take on this challenge.

Decide what steps need to be taken to make it better or fix it.

Look for anything you can take away from it that is helpful.

As you are going through it, look for ways to seek help.

Accepting a situation does not preclude taking action. By that I mean you don't just battle and claw your way out. You place yourself in a frame of mind that enables you to operate in a wise and beneficial manner.

#3. Take mindful action

Why not channel that energy into organized thought and then action since overthinking is typically a futile activity?

Do something uplifting to divert your attention from unpleasant ideas when your mind is cluttered. Anything that needs some thought and concentration will work, but we advise taking thoughtful action—an action that is focused on your beliefs, goals, or priorities.

Defining your goals, which we cover in the next part, is a straightforward method to accomplish this. Determining your beliefs and priorities for the upcoming year is actually one of the first thoughtful actions you may perform.

Some suggestions you could test out are as follows:

Writing

playing a musical instrument

building anything from scratch

Drawing or painting

working on a challenging issue

studying and memorization

developing a speech

creating something from nothing

All of these tasks involve concentration and some sort of mental effort, which helps keep you from reverting to mindless worrying or overthinking.

#4. Establish a worry timer.

The habit of worrying cannot be totally broken. There will be times when your mind is so overtaken by negative thoughts that no amount of self-talk or diversion will be able to stop you.

You don't have to dive headfirst into the quagmire of pessimistic thinking, though, even in these circumstances. You can control how much time you spend thinking so that you don't get stuck there and find it difficult to surface.

Set a timer for 10 to 15 minutes, then permit yourself to worry about everything that comes to mind. Release all of it! Use this opportunity to release all of your suppressed emotions and thoughts. You might keep a journal during your "worry time" and record your ideas there. Longhand writing aids in cognitive processing and frequently results in original problem-solving ideas.

As advised in the prior technique, stand up when the timer goes off and do something diverting to help you wind down this worrying period. If you discover that one anxiety session is insufficient, schedule another for the morning and another for the afternoon. In between sessions, when you find yourself drifting back into your thoughts, remind yourself to wait until the next one.

Last Thoughts on decluttering your thoughts

These techniques for teaching your mind to function more productively may not be used by you, but they provide you with a variety of options so you are ready. To lessen concern and overthinking, I had discovered that the capacity to question thoughts and see how they frequently don't correspond to reality is especially useful. You'll learn which of these techniques fits you and the mental clutter that frequently fills your attention the best. If you catch yourself reverting to old habits, don't give up. You must regularly practice any new behavior before it becomes second nature.

Chapter 4

Cognitive Restructuring

Most people occasionally have negative thought patterns, but occasionally these patterns can become so ingrained that they affect relationships, success, and even well-being.

A collection of therapeutic strategies known as cognitive restructuring aids in identifying and modifying unfavorable thought patterns.

It's a good idea to look into methods for interrupting and rerouting thought patterns when they start to become negative and self-defeating. Cognitive restructuring is capable of accomplishing this. Cognitive restructuring is concerned with identifying and altering unfavorable self-statements and learner beliefs. Building an adapted mindset is the goal of putting cognitive restructuring strategies into practice. The goal of cognitive restructuring is to pinpoint and correct people's cognitive biases or misconceptions about the world around them.

Negative self-statements are a form of cognitive mistake. Self-deprecating statements reveal illogical ideas, opinions, and beliefs.

A maladaptive person's incorrect thought process affects their behavior or emotions Self-criticism can be used to discover thinking mistakes and begin the cognitive restructuring process. After then, start to change your mind by rejecting the criticism.

Given that many of our problems stem from faulty ways of thinking about ourselves and our surroundings, it is a cornerstone of cognitive behavioral therapy and a strategy widely used in a therapist's repertoire. The cognitive restructuring aims to help people reduce stress by developing more constructive and beneficial thought processes. Though it might seem impossible, it is actually similar to learning any other skill: it is challenging when you first start, but with practice, you will find that challenging your own unfavorable thoughts and beliefs becomes easier and easier.

What part does cognitive rehabilitation play in behavioral therapy?
The foundation of cognitive behavioral therapy, or CBT, is the notion that our thoughts and feelings are interconnected. The reasoning behind this notion and the results of erroneous thinking is simple to understand.

When CBT and REBT were first developed, cognitive restructuring was used as a therapeutic strategy. Practitioners of CBT soon discovered that it was a versatile and adaptable approach that could assist a wide spectrum of people facing a variety of problems, whether the problems were brought on by internal or external forces, or both.

The majority of CBT sessions are devoted to this approach to problem-solving and healing, which includes a variety of exercises and techniques that can be used in almost any client situation. If used appropriately, it will teach the client to start questioning the veracity of his or her thoughts rather than reflexively accepting them as accurate representations of reality.

Overgeneralization, Magnification, and Other Cognitive Distortions

It almost comes as a surprise that we think more logically most of the time given how many ways our thinking may deceive us! Psychology refers to these ruses as "cognitive distortions."

Cognitive distortions are flawed or partial ways of understanding ourselves and/or our surroundings. These are unfounded, incorrect, or unreasonable ideas and thought patterns that can seriously harm our sense of self, our confidence, and our capacity for success.

Magnification or minimization, a harmful distortion that impacts how we assess the things that happen to us, is one of the most prevalent cognitive distortions.

Cognitive Restructuring Techniques

Fortunately, despite the fact that cognitive distortions are persistent and deceptive mental processes, there are strategies to combat them! Cognitive restructuring approaches have proven very successful in identifying, testing, and replacing erroneous ways of thinking with more precise, helpful, and positive ways of thinking.

Raising Thinking Awareness

Identifying your flawed thinking is the first step toward correcting it. A crucial step in this process is raising your awareness of your own ideas, especially those excessively unfavorable or biased ones.

Your ability to become more conscious of your own thoughts will take practice and time. People don't usually pause and reflect on how they got to where they are while they are going through a strong feeling.

Start by activating your internal "radar" for negative emotions to look for cognitive distortions. Consider the times when your symptoms of despair, anxiety, or rage are most severe. Start with your behaviors if starting with your emotions is too challenging. Determine what prompts the behaviors you would like to modify in yourself by asking yourself what those behaviors are.

These circumstances can be thought of as "alarm" circumstances, or circumstances that make you aware of the existence of one or more cognitive distortions.

Examples of alarm circumstances include:
Before heading out with pals, you start to feel anxious. You sweat and your heart beats quickly.

After meeting with your boss, you start arguing with your partner. Every disagreement begins with a small issue, like chores. You wait until the very last minute to do a significant task when it is due at school. There is no issue with little assignments.

When you have to spend the night by yourself, you experience depression. You can't stand how lonely you feel.

Think about these alarming circumstances and then imagine similar circumstances in your own life. Exist any situations that commonly cause unpleasant or painful feelings? Do particular circumstances have an outsized influence on your mood?

Make an effort to pinpoint as many triggering circumstances as you can; the more specific they are, the better. While starting your cognitive restructuring work, having a list of your most frequent or important triggers is tremendously helpful.

Socratic Questioning

You or your customers can use the cognitive restructuring approach known as Socratic inquiry to confront erroneous, damaging, or unreasonable thought patterns.

The following questions should be asked as the fundamental outline for this technique:

Is this idea plausible?

Do I base my opinions on facts or on emotions?

What support does this idea have?

Might I be interpreting the data incorrectly?

Do I have a simplistic picture of the problem when it's actually more nuanced?

Do the facts support my thought, or am I just thinking it out of habit?

Our minds constantly have a conversation going on, but it can happen so quickly that we hardly have time to comprehend them, let alone respond to them.

Finding the concepts you believe need to be challenged is the first step. Consider a particular thought that you believe to be negative or unreasonable, preferably one that frequently enters your mind.

Next, think about the arguments in favor of and against this assertion. What evidence exists to support this assumption? What proof is there that casts doubt on it?

You can reach a conclusion regarding this idea once you have identified the supporting evidence. Determine whether the thought is more likely to be true or untrue by weighing the evidence for and against it. Identify whether it is founded on the truth or your emotions. You then respond to a question on whether this issue is actually black and white or whether there are some gray areas in reality. Here, you should consider whether you are utilizing all-or-nothing reasoning or simplifying issues that are actually quite complex.

The Cognitive Restructuring Process in 5 Stages (CR)

When you're worried or distressed about anything, you can use this skill to carefully examine your thoughts. It can be applied to any circumstance when you are feeling unfavorable emotions. If a careful assessment of an unpleasant thought proves to be inaccurate, you'll switch to a thought that is correct and less upsetting. If your assessment shows that you're

105

distressed, If your train of thought is sound, you'll develop an action plan to cope with the circumstance.

Step 1: The situation

Step 1 involves writing down the upsetting circumstance. The circumstance might actually occur, such as visiting the grocery store, arguing with someone, or recalling

an occurrence like reflecting on the calamity. Just write one sentence in any scenario explaining the circumstance.

Step 2: The emotion

The second step is to pinpoint the most distressing emotion you experienced.

There are occasions when you may have experienced multiple emotions, yet you should concentrate on determining the emotion that is most intense and distressing. It's simplest to concentrate on

Four general emotions

• Anxiety and terror

• Depression and sadness

• Shame and regret

• anger

Choose one of these four emotions, and use it to guide you through all five processes.
For instance, fear may be the main emotion felt before heading to the grocery shop.

Fill out a CR on the situation if you feel strongly about more than one thing, The first feeling, followed by another CR on the following feeling.

Step 3 : The thought

Step 3 asks you to pinpoint the ideas about the circumstance that are driving your feelings. distressing emotions. If you're not sure what those thoughts are, pose the following questions to yourself.

Depending on how you felt, ask the following questions:

• While experiencing fear or anxiety, consider: "What unpleasant thing am I anticipating happening?" What sort of risk am I in?

• When feeling sad or depressed, consider "What have I lost hope in?" "How is
missing from my life or myself?

• While feeling guilty or ashamed, consider your recent transgressions. What's wrong with me?"

• When you feel angry, consider what is unfair about the circumstance. "Who has wronged me?"

These questions can assist you in identifying the thoughts that are bothering you. Anxiety about going to the grocery store, for example, may be related to the thinking "I won't be able to get out if someone starts shooting;" Feeling guilty for not escaping sooner could be linked to the notion "If I had evacuated sooner, I would have saved my father's life."

When identifying distressing ideas, try to be as explicit as possible. For example, "There may be a gunman in the grocery shop and I wouldn't be able to get out alive" is more precise than "Something horrible could happen in the grocery store."Similarly, the idea "I would have been able to save my father's life if I had fled sooner" is more precise than the thought "I am a wicked person."

You might be thinking a lot of disturbing things about the circumstance. The ensuing inquiries may aid in identifying other troubling ruminations regarding the circumstance:

• If XX occurred, what would it mean to you?

• What would happen if XX occurred?

• Why would XX happening be so bad?

Fill out the worksheet with all of your troubling thoughts regarding the scenario. When you're finished, go through each thought and chose the one that upsets or distresses you the most. On the worksheet, circle the thought that you will be working on for the next several steps.

Consider whether your most distressing thought is one of the Problematic Thinking Types listed on the worksheet. That is, consider whether your thinking is a typical but incorrect way of obtaining a conclusion in a scenario. The notion "There could be a gunman at the grocery store and I wouldn't be able to get out alive" is an example of the Overestimating Risk thinking style. If you believe your thinking is related to one (or more) of the Problematic Thinking Styles above, circle the ones that you believe it is. If not, or if you are doubtful, do not circle any of them.

Step 4: Evaluate the thoughts.

Step 4 involves carefully and objectively assessing the accuracy of your disturbing thinking. To begin, consider all of the information that supports your thought or leads you to believe it is correct. For instance, in response to the idea "There could be a gunman in the grocery shop and I wouldn't be able to get out alive," a person could inquire, "Why do I think there would be a shooter at the grocery store?" "And why do I think I wouldn't be able to get out alive if there was a shooter there?" Fill up the worksheet with all of the evidence. Then, consider all of the evidence that contradicts or suggests your hypothesis is incorrect. Explore as many possibilities as you can for why your initial thinking was incorrect. Finally, on the worksheet, record all of the evidence against the thought.

Going back to Step 3 and re-evaluating if you decided that the notion might be a Problematic Thinking Style will assist you to come up with evidence that refutes the thought. If you answered affirmatively and circled one or more of the specific Problematic Thinking Styles, it indicates that you believe the thought might be false. You can then reflect on your reasoning for holding that belief. If for instance, the person identifying the thought about the shooter in Step 3 indicated that it was an example of the Overestimating Risk thinking style, they could then ask themselves, "Does thinking that a shooter could be in the grocery store overestimate the real chances of such a thing occurring?" and "How likely is it that a shooter will show up at the supermarket when I go shopping?"

Responses to these queries serve as proof that the thought is not true and should be noted.

Asking yourself the following questions can help you spot evidence that contradicts a particular idea.

Questions that could lead to new perspectives on the circumstance and your own thinking. a few good

You should inquire about:

1. Is there another angle from which to view the circumstances?

2. Is there a different account of what transpired?

3. What other perspectives might the situation elicit?

4. Is my worry driven more by my emotions than by the situation's actual facts?

5. Am I holding myself to impossible standards that I could never meet?

expect others to accomplish?

6. Am I exaggerating my degree of influence and accountability here?

situation?

7. What would be the worst scenario if my fear came true?

8. Have I thought of every possible solution to the issue or circumstance?

9. Am I assuming that because an unlikely event happened to me, it must be true?

very likely to occur to me once more?

The individual gave the following example of presenting all the arguments for and against a thought:

The following information might be used to assess the veracity of the statement "There could be a gunman at the grocery store and I wouldn't be able to get out alive."

• Public locations can be the scene of shootings.

• I felt scared.

• A man wearing a backpack that might have contained a weapon was at the shop.

• It would be difficult to leave if there was a shooting without standing out.

Then the individual might cite the following arguments against the thought:

• Nothing untoward has occurred on any of my several trips to the grocery shop.

• Even when nothing awful happens, I frequently feel terrified.

• Just because a man was carrying a backpack doesn't guarantee he was armed.

• Mass shootings in public settings, such as supermarkets, are extremely rare, and such an

quite unlikely to occur.

Step 5: Choose your action

Making a decision as to whether your thought is accurate or not is the fifth step.

on every piece of information, you stated in Step 4, making a decision, and then acting on that decision. While weighing the evidence for and against the veracity of your hypothesis, you should give more weight to strong, objective, fact-based evidence and less weight to weak, subjective, or belief-based evidence.

Being objective when assessing your thought is crucial because you want to have the most accurate grasp of the issue possible so that any actions you take are well-informed and successful.

You can imagine yourself as a scientist who is assessing the evidence demonstrating the efficacy of a novel treatment and is primarily concerned with objective facts when attempting to be objective.

Or, you could imagine yourself as a lawyer who is presenting the facts to a fair jury while arguing for or against a case. You might also contemplate whether you could persuade someone else that the idea is accurate (or false).

For instance, the person might have judged that the idea that a shooter would be present at the grocery shop was erroneous after considering the facts for and against it("There may be a shooter in the grocery store, and I wouldn't get out alive"). The fact that the person had gone to the grocery store numerous times previously and nothing had happened, the prevalence of backpacks without concealed weapons, and the rarity of mass shootings in public areas were the strongest arguments against the theory.

You take appropriate action in accordance with your choice after determining whether the notion is true or false (and checking the appropriate box on the worksheet). If you came to the conclusion that the evidence did not support the notion, you then replaced your previous faulty thought with a new and more accurate one. The worksheet is updated to reflect this fresh idea. Compared to the original, faulty notion, new and more accurate thoughts are almost always linked to a decrease in distress.

Chapter 5

Narrative Therapy

According to the theory behind narrative therapy, the details and delivery of our stories might help us understand how others live their lives. Nevertheless, only half of narrative therapy involves storytelling. Retelling, or working with a narrative therapist to retell your story in a way that gives you control over the issue, is the second phase.

Following their 1981 encounter at an Australian New Zealander family therapy conference, social workers Michael White and David Epston jointly developed story therapy. The foundation of narrative therapy is the belief that our unique life experiences can shed important light on how we behave and interact with the world around us.

The Art of Storytelling

Many individuals overlook how intricate and frequently fascinating one's life events are.

Many people's minds have been so negatively conditioned by sound bites that they begin to think of their own stories in this way. The oppression of mainstream culture is represented by those who are inclined to such crude descriptions (blaming, criticism, labeling) for their acts or self-identities (which they have produced or which others may have constructed for them by others). Such self-descriptions leave little room for the particularities, complexities, and inconsistencies of life. They frequently serve as superficial explanations, a pathologizing (causal labeling) abstract, if you will, that might hide true emotions, intentions, attitudes, goals, and the wide range of complicated human emotions and relationships. Such shallow tales frequently produce thin judgments and poor descriptions of potential issues. It's common for people to name themselves or receive labels like "bad," "a troublemaker," "looser," or "lazy."

Such labels (thin descriptions) can sometimes obscure positive traits and conceal a more detailed picture of a person's life that could have and ought to have been presented.

Those who learn to generate rich and thick descriptions are frequently able to discern alternate storylines or unique outcomes having very different effects than the thin ones they frequently meet on a daily basis, either through instruction or self-learning. The expression of minute details from a person's life narratives is a key component of rich descriptions of one's experiences. A person can write his or her own richly detailed narrative, which might inspire fresh, innovative approaches to solving issues.

Certain personal narratives could benefit from having a friend or coach as a co-author who can provide clarification, active listening, and reflection.

It can be uplifting to have a better understanding of how to rewrite troublesome life stories. We can observe a process by which people select their favorite versions and interpretations of their stories from a vast array of experiences and exciting occurrences that are also a part of their stories but have historically received less attention. Viable solution understandings (knowing what one might accomplish) and personal resources that are more readily incorporated into a rich life story and a new sense of self may lead to new options. By including the specifics and details of the major and minor themes in one's life, the story can be made more compelling and one can gain a deeper understanding of the richness of their own life.

The process of narrating:
The first step in the narrative process is to define a problem within its social context before starting the externalization process. When a problem is externalized, people are frequently able to distance themselves from it and are better equipped to come up with alternate explanations for how they relate to the problem personally. When problems are externalized, they become less ingrained in "who the person is" and have less of a solid foundation. When someone is able to see another perspective on the problem and

switches from speaking of the problem as it is to speaking of it as an influence or in relation to it (the externalized influence), they frequently discover that there are significantly more stories for problem solutions emerging from the four-front.

Items like emotions, interpersonal conflicts, cultural and social norms, anxieties, addictions, and other maladies can be externalized. Every externalized story focuses on issues that are external to people and the effects they have on them. What impact do "the fear," "the addiction," "the anger or guilt," or "the depression" have on how you go about your regular business? By personifying or using the problem area as a metaphor, a rich story might raise concerns about the problem's strategies, tactics, mode of operation, goals, beliefs and ideas, plans, or whatever keeps it around. Its guidelines, aspirations, drives, tactics, and lies or deceptions are investigated as it goes about its filthy business.

It may be useful to comprehend why one should be able to externalize problems as many people are specialists at doing so. It might also shed light on the reasons why discussing problems in public might lead to more creative solutions and the discovery of new material for stories that are still in the making. Examining the problem's past as well as the environments in which it formed, evolved, and currently dwells allows for the examination of other possible narratives. When a problem is examined over time, it frequently becomes less static and more dynamic, having varying degrees of impact on a person's life depending on the circumstances. It can be very helpful to investigate the origins of the issues and how they currently affect the person's life in a variety of contexts, such as their self-perception, how they see themselves in different roles, their hopes and dreams, their work and social life, their spirituality, their moods, and daily activities. It's also a good idea to inquire about the effects the condition has had on the person's life. One might also wonder why the person views the issue the way they do when it works or does not work when it manifests itself, and when it does not.

Redirecting and restaging the issue

The ideas, beliefs, values, and behaviors supported by prevailing cultural discourses, as well as their impact on the physical self and surroundings, are what enable problems to persist. The role of the helper is to assist in restructuring the problem story so that it is based on the beliefs, ideas, and practices of the larger culture in which the problem story occurs while also highlighting the impact of the person's preferences, hopes, dreams, ideas, and values in relation to the problem.

Problematic narratives, particularly those embedded deeply in the cement, need to be replaced with others that have a rich context and include numerous points of view from various sources. Events that were in opposition to the problem's influence must be mentioned. Other narratives might be built on the basis of these stunning results. These unusual results could be the result of previous or present activities that deviated from the norm, or they could be the result of a shift in one's plans, actions, feelings, what they said, the caliber of their work, desires or dreams, thoughts, beliefs, commitment, talents, or abilities. Thin histories (stories) frequently ignore these divergences from the dominant narrative because they tend to concentrate on what is obvious, the dominant theme, rather than the subtle aberration, no matter how beneficial it may have been. Texts rife with issues overshadow anything positive. Search for the silver linings that surround the ominous clouds.

How have you managed to prevent the issue from getting worse?

• What are the instances when the issue is manageable?

• How do you handle situations where the challenge must not get in the way?

• What types of things do you value more than your issue and when have you trusted your instincts and not allowed the issue to stand in your way?

The Alternate Story

The investigation of potential outcomes may open the way to brand-new and distinctive narratives about the lives and interactions of individuals. In order to modify people's behavior in the future, it is possible to bring unique outcomes to the forefront of people's awareness and match their capacity for re-creating them in new narratives. The specifics of the unusual result must be historically rich in terms of the environment, circumstances, actions, and results.

Detail exploration of sequential events, including results, is necessary. When crafting the new plot, it is important to investigate potential obstacles to continuing the unusual outcomes.

The following information about the exploration may also be included but is not limited to:

• Preferences, wishes, and desires

• Individual values

• Connectional traits

• Individual talents and skills

• Goals, plans, intentions, and justifications

• Values and beliefs

• Characteristics

An alternative story with a different plot could emerge as studies of the unique outcome in connection to the aforementioned variable advance (meanings). The subject may be questioned about personal traits they possess that would not surprise a loved one in the building of their new story. Looking for:

• Reasons

• Other people's opinions about the character

• Fresh perspectives

• Information about what someone else thought, felt and did can add flavor to a growing narrative and make it more engaging.

Once a different narrative has been developed, it should be given a label, such as "strength and survival" rather than "worthlessness." The moment is right for further in-depth detailing of the new narrative now that one has both positive and negative stories with them named in front of them.

Strengthening the Alternate Narrative

A number of strengthening techniques are used when replacing a current (sometimes problematic) tale with an alternative story. These steps can be used in any order that the person and any helping professionals, such as a therapist or assistant, choose.

• Acquiring witnesses and a readership for the fresh account. Many support groups for all kinds of human illnesses are built on this principle.

• Enriching the presentation of the alternative new story with recollected talks. Who would use their own interactions with the person to support the new story? This is a way to connect with crucial social support from the past, the present, and the future. These memories could be connected or unconnected, real or made up, and could involve pets, animals, places, symbols, or items.

Find (remember) people who would share the same preferences, commitments, beliefs, or values as the new story and use reciprocal sharing or connection to their life. The reciprocal is equally effective when you ask the person being recalled what significance their friend's recollection has for them and how it has changed them.

• Use documents, declarations, certificates, notes, videos, lists, and images to create therapeutic documentation of significant accomplishments relating to the new story.

• Develop the skill of writing therapeutic letters to loved ones, particularly the

therapist. The healthcare professional, therapist, or support person will frequently serve as an example of this letter-writing and can help name the issue and its history, summarize the development to date, and validate and name newly reported tales.

• Include fresh celebrations and rituals in the fresh narrative.

• Identify a group of people who will support your new narrative, and have that narrative reinforced on a regular basis.

Chapter 6

Time and input management

Good time management is good stress management for many of us. You might benefit more from time management tactics than relaxing approaches if you frequently feel rushed, overwhelmed, stressed out, or nervous about deadlines. The key to effective time management is to recognize your priorities and use them as a guide when setting goals. As usual, the mind is everything.

When you consider how many of us value stress in our lives, it's strange. We devote all of our free time to pursuits that aggravate our emotions and leave us exhausted or nervous. When was the last time you gave relaxation a high priority? If you're like most people, you always prioritize your hard work while giving anything else only crumbs of your time and attention.

One way to change your perspective is to stop thinking of relaxation as something you do at the end of the day after you've finished more pressing matters. Making time for delightful activities and times when you do nothing at all is one method to do this. Why not actively care for and cultivate these happy emotions since a cheerful attitude is one of your most significant resources in life?

Instead of starting the day with tedious jobs and chores, you may do something enjoyable. Make it a routine to take a ten-minute break every hour to stretch, enjoy a cup of herbal tea, or go for a short stroll. Develop relationships with individuals you care about and who brighten your life so that you have something to look forward to each day. Spend a little time having fun, making jokes, and doing something just because it makes you happy.

You already know what lifestyle modifications you need to do to take care of your bodily needs and reduce stress, such as getting enough sleep, cutting back on your caffeine use, exercising, eating right, and so on. Your social, emotional, and spiritual well-being is also significant. Some tasks just won't be completed if you don't take the time to perform them.

Time management is more than just a quick approach to managing your daily tasks. It's a way to organize your entire life and control how you live so that you may focus your time, money, and energy on the really important things. Balance and view your life with the understanding that its proportions and priorities reflect your values are more important than simply cramming as much work into a day as you can.

Let's face it: there will always be something fresh vying for your attention and taking up your time. To make the most of the time and energy we have, it is up to us to consciously direct the course of life. This is an excellent general foundation for doing this:

1. Decide on your values and priorities in life. What three things mean most to you?

2. Track how you use the time you have available for a week. Keep a log of your activities for each hour.

3. Examine this information to determine your preferred location. And the worst time? Check to discover if your actual time management

practices align with your ideals. Does it make sense, for instance, to spend 90% of your waking hours working alone if your top priorities are your family, starting your own business, and remaining in shape?

4. Rearrange your schedule to more accurately reflect your priorities, guided by your values and principles.

5. Re-observe to assess your performance, what is working, and any necessary corrections.

Without understanding your priorities and goals, there is no value in discussing time management. Knowing what you value first is essential to effective time management because it completely depends on the results you're looking for. You can begin to decide what is important and what isn't by ranking activities and chores with your values in mind.

Start each day with your top priorities, which receive the majority of your focus, time, and resources. Create a daily to-do list in the morning. Go over the items and decide whether they are urgent, important, or not important.

Things that need to be done right away should be given priority. Delaying these invites stress. Essential jobs are a little less urgent, and they frequently involve "life maintenance" chores like bringing out the trash that, if neglected, can lead to issues.

Tasks that are not vital can wait or are not given priority. You can create your rating system and define what is truly important to you, but make sure you are clear on it before you assign each label to a task. Some people find it helpful to focus on just a few urgent or significant activities each day, so they ask themselves, "What three things am I going to focus on today?" They then unwind while working on other, less important tasks.

There are several helpful tools and ways created to help speed the process as well as numerous time management ideas, approaches, and strategies. Yet, if you adhere to the aforementioned principles, you may make your time work for you. There are a few things to bear in mind, but an effective time management habit will reflect your lifestyle and objectives: Have a physical to-do list, calendar, schedule, or other physical items where you can record your daily goals and track your progress. Writing things down makes them more concrete.

You'll accomplish more over time if you concentrate on everyday positive habits as opposed to immediate outcomes and perfectionism.

Become used to declining offers that are not important. It's acceptable to assign tasks or set boundaries so that people respect your boundaries.

Always compare your current course of action to your larger objectives and ask yourself: Is this moving me closer or further away? then take appropriate action.

Naturally, presenting it in this manner makes time management look straightforward, and while it is simple, it is not always easy. Even if we know better, we occasionally cling to negative behavioral tics from the past. But if we are aware of these obstacles, we can avoid them and plan ahead for them. Why do some time management strategies work better than others for different people? Why? Well, because no two people are alike and no one faces the same difficulties.

Individual time management personas or styles exist in addition to time management strategies. The time martyr, for instance, is the person who agrees to everyone else's requests and assumes too much responsibility before paying the price. If this describes you, being so busy may give you a false sense of pride because you are not focusing on the things that are truly important to you. Anything that reduces multitasking and distractions, such as a rigid schedule or the requirement to finish no more than three major activities each day, would be beneficial for you.

Many difficulties face the procrastinator, who frequently puts off taking any action until it is already too late. While little pressure can be beneficial, procrastinators are worse off when they feel anxious. If you procrastinate, it could help to divide the work into smaller jobs and give yourself rewards as you complete each mini-milestone.

A similar issue affects the distractor; they start but are frequently sidetracked by them and find their focus wandering. Having stricter limits and paying more attention to the type of workplace environment they work in are effective strategies for those with this propensity. The underestimator makes the error of anticipating that tasks will take less time than they actually do, and they may miss deadlines as a result. However, time management also involves planning to tackle assignments gradually so that you have the time to evaluate the process realistically. When a situation has reached a crisis, the firefighter is frequently in a reactive mindset, putting out "fires" everywhere and juggling a thousand things at once. Such a person could improve their delegation skills and their ability to differentiate between urgent and essential tasks to avoid burnout. Rushing to find solutions all the time may indicate that you are not taking the proper action in the beginning and are allowing things to get out of hand until they are much more difficult to handle.

Like the procrastinator, the perfectionist never completes tasks because nothing ever measures up to their ideal result. The reality is that perfectionism frequently masks a fear of completion or an intolerance of "good enough" results that occur along a learning curve. Setting limits, making practical plans, and delegating can all be helpful.

It's important to recognize how you are acting right now so you may take efforts to change, whether you identify with one or more of the aforementioned traits or discover that your time management style is something entirely different. Observe trends and consider what is now preventing you from managing your time more effectively. Any time management approach is only helpful if it is effective for you in your daily life.

How to Control Your Energy, Time, and Inputs

Let's take a deeper look at some of the techniques that could assist you in overcoming your particular time management challenges. You could give the following a try while taking your lifestyle and personal time management style into consideration.

SMART Goal Setting

You're undoubtedly already aware of the idea that effective objectives are those that are both specific and time-bound or so-called SMART goals. Someone who is unsure of their path and their ideals is more likely to feel overwhelmed and nervous even under modest stress levels, whereas someone who is certain of what they want and why they want it might appear to dig deep and persevere through great obstacles and failures.

We are aware of how goals can sift through confusion and distraction to bring order and focus to our lives. But having a strong sense of your values does not necessarily translate into effective goal-setting. Make deliberate efforts to ensure that you are establishing the right kinds of goals that are most likely to be accomplished. SMART goals serve as a road map from where you are to where you want to be:

S stands for particular. By definition, this lessens distractions. Be as explicit as you can. Don't just predict what will happen; be specific about what you will do.

M stands for Measurable. A good objective can be measured or quantified. The conclusion is unambiguous. How will I know when my goal has been attained?

A stands for accomplishable. This indicates that it is practical for you given your circumstances. A goal should push us to go further, but it also needs to be attainable and reasonable.

R stands for Relevant. Do your larger values align with this objective? Check to see if the smaller goal makes sense in relation to the larger one.

T stands for time-bound. Decide on a target date for completion or specify a time frame for completion. "Someday" goals are never achieved.

A goal that isn't particularly good is shown here: I desire to improve my health.

The same goal is stated below, and it has been written to meet all SMART requirements: "I want to consume five servings of fruit and vegetables every day, all various kinds,"

(i.e., each serving is 80g) in an effort to have a better diet overall. I want to keep up this diet every day for the rest of the month.

Here, the objective is defined (it's five different fruits and vegetables a day), measurable (we can track 80g), achievable (not overly ambitious), relevant (it makes sense for the overall objective of a better diet), and time-bound (it's daily, but it also lasts until the end of the month).

Now, SMART objectives don't alter how challenging the tasks you have ahead of you will be. Yet, they do assist you in developing and defining your vision so you can act more effectively. They encourage you to consider more thoroughly what and how you are doing. So many of us set out on missions with little knowledge of the specifics, only to let ourselves down as the plan suddenly fails.

A SMART goal is essentially a travel map from the present to the future, and any activity that has a clear and logical plan for it is bound to be more effective.

To truly write out your goals may seem apparent and clichéd, but if you do it, you could be astonished at how vague the vision is. If you make your goals a little more specific, you'll find that being more determined to carry out your plan comes from being more concentrated in your approach.

Time Blocking

Most of us spend a significant amount of time working each day.

But, it's so simple to lose time to meetings, emails, and other "busy stuff" that distracts you from what really matters and encourages overthinking. For those firefighters, procrastinators, and time martyrs who wish to control their work schedules to reduce stress, time blocking is fantastic. It can assist you in escaping the reactive, preoccupied state and averting days that feel jumbled, interrupted, or chaotic.

Instead of multitasking or quickly moving between tasks, time blocking involves allocating certain blocks of time in your schedule to one activity and that task only. By making decisions in advance, you may avoid wasting time or willpower and guarantee that you always start with your priorities. Instead of paying shallow attention to several things at once, you want to promote "deep work" and become interested in what you're doing. This is not only efficient (you accomplish more in a set amount of time), but it is also significantly less stressful. You might accomplish more with less mental or emotional effort.

Although shallow work is all the other stuff the jobs you wish to outsource or completely get rid of deep work are everything in your "urgent and important" and "important but not urgent" chores. A good day is one in which you maximized the amount of time spent on the activities that enhance your life and assist you in achieving your goals while reducing the amount of shallow work you must complete and the aggravation it might cause.

Time blocking can help you control your perfectionist tendencies and get a more accurate sense of how long things take.

Start by considering your goals for the day or the week as well as your top priorities. This will direct how you go.

Next, consider the morning and evening routines you want to create at the beginning and conclusion of each day. For instance, you might begin with a morning workout and meditation and finish with a comforting book or family time. Of course, these are all set in accordance with your beliefs and priorities, as well as your particular sleeping and waking patterns. Next, schedule the most important things first, keeping them for when you'll be attentive and enthusiastic. Preserve these sections as intact as you can.

Include space in your schedule for shallower, less critical tasks, and plan for periods when you are not as productive.

Of course, you'll need a specific time each day for duties you can't properly plan, including replying to emails or other urgent matters. Make time to address things so they won't accumulate and cause you to stress. You can confidently disregard reactive jobs that fall outside of their specified window now that you have a predetermined time for them.

Examine your schedule, then give it a try for a few days. It's not gospel—change what doesn't work after observing what does.

Many people arrange specific periods for leisure and rest, and they make sure there is some time between each work just in case. To avoid feeling like it's all or nothing, you might also like to designate one day a week to catch up or "overflow."

Remember that your schedule is designed to assist you in maintaining control; it does not control you. Adjust something if it isn't working. Test out various calendars, reminders, and schedule-management applications. Try using longer or shorter blocks, and consider including a daily break where you pause to evaluate how you performed and why. Your timetable may eventually turn into one of your most effective stress-reduction tools, not to mention that it can significantly increase your productivity.

David Allen Processing Technique

The input processing method developed by David Allen is a framework that aids in the organization of activities, ideas, and projects.

The five easy steps of the Getting Things Done system are input, process, organize, review, and engage.

Picture yourself returning from work on foot. ecstatic that another good day has ended.

Nevertheless, you suddenly remember that it is Sam's birthday today and that you didn't call him. Yet, you were so busy the entire day that you were unable to call.

"No problem," you say to yourself."As soon as I get home, I'll wish him a happy birthday."Nevertheless, when you arrive home, a stack of unread mail and dirty dishes await you, and you are preoccupied with other tiresome housework.

How could something so crucial slip my mind, you think the following morning, feeling like a terrible friend? The explanation is straightforward: Your brain is designed to generate ideas, not to store them.

Things are bound to fall through the gaps with a never-ending stream of demands for your attention, both at home and at work.

You can only accomplish effective achievements when your mind is clear and your thoughts are well-organized.

Here, the Getting Things Done method abbreviated GTD comes into play. It is a system created to make it easier for you to manage chores, ideas, and projects.

The five easy steps of the Getting Things Done method are input, process, organize, review, and engage.

Input

It starts with "collecting" all of the random ideas, tasks, projects, to-do items, and other bits of information that come your way every day.

They could be communication-related items like emails, letters, calls, and action items, or they could be tasks and ideas that you come up with on your own.

You need to input or externalize the information, regardless of where it came from, so you won't have to keep it in your head.

Now that you've gathered all this knowledge, it's time to make sense of it so you can really move toward your objectives rather than feeling the need to take your heart out from the information overload.

Processing

Processing is step two in the GTD process.

The following inquiry should be asked of each item you enter: Is it actionable? There are just two options: YES or NO.

If the item is actionable, such as an email from a coworker asking you for an update on the project you are working on, consider whether it would take two minutes or less to complete. If the response is "yes," proceed with caution. If "no," you should postpone taking this action and list it as an action item instead.

Or if it will take you 30 seconds to reply to your colleague's email, it makes sense to take care of it on the spot and move on. It is best to schedule a 20-minute conversation if you need to discuss the matter.

If the item you are processing is "not actionable," such as a confirmation of a payment you made for your monthly internet bill, you have two options: discard it or keep it as a reference in case you need that information in the future. For every piece of information, carry out the same procedure.

Now that you've processed the information, things are starting to look up for you. You just need to organize it. The magic happens here. You have a list of all the things you need to do that are still actionable that you haven't already done.

Organize

Now you must arrange and rank them according to the three criteria listed below: project, time, and context.

Building a deck for your upcoming presentation or planning your kids' Halloween party are two examples of actions that might be grouped because they are linked to the same project. Actions that are time-sensitive or have a deadline of some kind are listed on your calendar so you can attend to them as necessary. Actions can also be grouped according to their context, such as calls you need to make or groceries you need to get. Of course, you can combine and place items in more than one category

This is where you must adjust and customize GTD to suit your requirements. In your opinion, How to organize and rank your stuff?

What is the next action is a thought you should retain in the forefront of your thoughts at all times. You are not being very efficient if you sit down to contact Sam on his birthday but don't have his phone number.

Instead of calling Sam, the next step should have been to "get Sam's number." The inquiry will assist you in better sequencing your actions.

Now that you've arranged your action items, the world is a happier place, the sun is beaming brightly. What about the issues that cannot be taken action on? That's simple, They can be stored for reference like that TV handbook, you don't need it until your child turns on the Spanish closed captioning and you have to figure out how to reverse it.

Perhaps they can be put off for later, such as that company idea you want to keep and explore in six months when you have more time; add it to a "someday maybe" list.

list and make a task to revisit it in six months. Done! High fives! You are now prepared to rule the world after organizing all the random information.

Review

Things will inevitably get out of order when there are so many demands on your time. This is when the review is useful. Review your items each week, and if necessary, make any necessary revisions.

Is everything in its proper place? Do you have a ton of information that has huge be processed? It's imperative to conduct a weekly review to keep everything in working order. Spend some time reviewing your short-term objectives each month.

Are you making progress toward your goals with your action items, or are you only keeping yourself busy?

Are you in reaction mode or saving up for that car you want? What about learning Spanish? To make sure the train is moving in the right direction, schedule these routine reviews and reflection times.

Engage

Engage is the name of the final element of the GTD process. Here's where you actually do your work clothes and get to work. All the chores you have to complete today should be listed on your calendar.

Also, your project list will outline the steps necessary to advance each project. You can group things with the aid of your contexts.

The following information will inevitably reach you as you go about your day and cross each thing off your list.

You now know what to do with it: record it, determine whether it is actionable, and then either take action if you can do it in less than two minutes or add it to the relevant action list if you can't. If the information cannot be used, it is either archived or discarded. Nothing to do about it.

You have reached the state of serenity and composure of a Zen Buddhist master who is deep in meditation.

Sam won't have to celebrate his birthday without receiving wishes from his best friend ever again!

Eisenhower Matrix

The first step to finishing work is to create a to-do list. So when you don't have enough time to complete everything in one day, how do you decide what to work on first? You can boost your productivity and guarantee that your most critical tasks receive prompt attention by prioritizing well.

An effective workflow can be established by using the Eisenhower Matrix, a task management tool, to distinguish between urgent and significant jobs. This post will outline the Eisenhower Matrix setup process and offer task prioritization advice.

The Eisenhower Matrix: What is it?

In order to successfully prioritize your most critical work, you can categorize activities according to urgency and importance using the Eisenhower Matrix.

Dwight D. Eisenhower, the 34th President of the United States and a five-star general during World War II, proposed the Eisenhower Matrix. In a 1954 address, Eisenhower quoted an anonymous university president as saying, "I have two sorts of problems: urgent and significant." The urgent is never important, and the important is never urgent.

The Eisenhower Box, the time management matrix, and the urgent-important matrix are further names for the Eisenhower Matrix. This tool aids in categorizing your jobs into four groups: those you'll complete first; those you'll schedule for later; those you'll assign; and those you'll eliminate.

How to tell the difference between important and urgent work Although urgent and important may seem to have identical meanings, the Eisenhower principle makes it clear that there is a significant distinction between the two. Inside the Eisenhower Matrix, separating urgent activities from significant ones will help you decide which duties you should take on right away and which ones other team members would be better suited to tackle.

Tasks that need your immediate attention are urgent. When something is essential, it needs to be done right away, and failing to finish these chores by the deadline will have obvious repercussions. You cannot escape these activities, and the longer you put off completing them, the more stressed you will likely become, which may result in burnout.

These are a few examples of urgent tasks:

completing a task with a short deadline

addressing a pressing client request

repair of a leaking pipe in your flat

Even if they may not need your immediate attention, important chores are nevertheless necessary for your long-term success. These duties are nonetheless important even though they are less urgent. Planning these jobs carefully will be necessary to make the best use of your resources.

Important task examples include the following:

Creating a long-term project plan

building a clientele through professional networking

regular errands and maintenance tasks

You can start organizing your work into the four quadrants of the Eisenhower Matrix once you understand how to differentiate between urgent and significant jobs.

The Eisenhower Matrix's four Quadrants

The Eisenhower Matrix aims to go through these tasks one at a time and separate them by quadrant. A long to-do list of tasks can seem overwhelming. You'll be able to schedule them and complete your most crucial duties once you can see your tasks in their designated categories.

Quadrant 1: Do

Any jobs that are both urgent and significant should be in the first quadrant, known as the "do" quadrant. Put an item on your to-do list in this quadrant if it needs to be done immediately, has obvious repercussions, and affects your long-term objectives.

The chores that go in this quadrant should be obvious as they are the ones that are on your mind and are probably causing you the greatest stress.

Quadrant 2: Schedule

The second quadrant, known as the "schedule" quadrant, is where you should place any tasks that are significant but not urgent. You can plan to complete these tasks later because they have an impact on your long-term goals but don't require immediate attention. Following your completion of the tasks in quadrant 1, you will begin working on these. The tasks in this quadrant can be completed with the use of a variety of time management strategies. The Pareto principle and the Pomodoro method are a couple of effective techniques.

Quadrant 3: Delegate

Any jobs that are urgent but not critical should go into the third quadrant, which is the "delegate" quadrant. These duties must be met right now, but they have no bearing on your long-term objectives.

You can assign these tasks to other members of your team because you don't feel a personal connection to them and they probably don't require your particular skill set to execute. One of the most effective strategies to manage your workload is to assign responsibilities to your team, which also gives them the chance to grow as a team.

Quadrant 4: Delete

You'll note that a few things are still outstanding after going through your to-do list and adding items to the first three quadrants. Tasks that weren't urgent or important are the ones that are still outstanding. You just can't fulfill your objectives if you are distracted by these irrelevant, non-urgent things. Put these last tasks on your to-do list in the fourth quadrant.

Four suggestions for setting priorities

Using the Eisenhower Matrix is the greatest way to distinguish between urgency and importance, but you might still struggle with job prioritization. Once you arrange your work into the four quadrants, the following advice can assist you in setting priorities.

Organize your projects by color.

You can use color coding to better understand your high-priority tasks. Try assigning yourself four colors based on priority as you go through your to-do list application. Use the following code:

Green denotes the most important items.

 yellow is the second-highest priority color.

Green is the Second-to-last priority

Red is not a priority

Your Eisenhower Matrix will automatically reflect the colors you use to name your tasks. For quadrant one, your green tasks are your "do" tasks. Your "schedule" tasks for quadrant two are those in the color yellow. For quadrants three and four, your blue tasks are your "delegate" tasks, and your red tasks are your "delete" tasks.

2. Limit the number of jobs to ten per quadrant.

Even if you have a long list of chores to complete, try to keep it to 10 items in each quadrant. This will keep your Eisenhower Matrix from becoming crowded and confusing.

You can create multiple matrices, but keeping your task list to essential items will guarantee that you can start the prioritization process right away.

Weary of putting off your tasks? 5 stages to master the GTD methodology

3. Create to-do lists for your work and personal life.

Using separate Eisenhower Matrixes for your personal and business to-do lists is another technique to reduce the number of items on your Eisenhower Matrix.

Your personal and professional duties will probably require different cognitive processes as well as different schedules, resources, and approaches. You'll need to divide and conquer to manage your personal and professional goals properly.

4. Prioritize after eliminating

Prioritize successfully by first eliminating superfluous tasks. By employing this method, you will address quadrant four before tackling quadrants one, two, and three.

Examine the items on your to-do list that don't need to be there as you scan it.

Work-related activities like exchanging status approvals or information follow-up take up 60% of our time at work. Scratch off items as soon as you can if you can. This will hasten the process of prioritization, and you'll probably have to go through a second round of elimination afterward.

Eisenhower Matrix illustration

We've gone ahead and given you some examples below so you can see what duties you might include in each quadrant of your Eisenhower Matrix.

You could perform the following tasks in Quadrant 1:

Prepare a blog entry for tomorrow.

Complete the project proposal.

Answering client emails

You could include the following tasks in Quadrant 2:

Enroll in a course for professional development

Go to a networking gathering

Increase the quality of a personal project.

You could perform the following actions in quadrant 3:

Publish blog entries

recording meeting minutes

receiving emails from people who are not clients

You could perform the following actions in quadrant 4:

job-related work

taking part in a status meeting

sharing approvals of status

Keep in mind that it's essential to have distinct matrices for your job and personal lives so you may complete your to-do lists according to the finest schedules and environments.

Conclusion

The mental equivalent of cleaning your house is training your mind. You have to practice it every day to keep on top of it. Nevertheless, mind training is not as easy or uncomplicated as cleaning.

Taking control of your thoughts requires dedication and effort. It also necessitates constant awareness of your mental state and the antics of your monkey mind, even on a moment-by-moment basis.

When left to its ways, your mind will wander, going after a distracting thought, an old memory, or the bitter juice of hatred or rage. Sometimes it can linger in considerably more uplifting but erratic mental states like daydreaming and fantasizing. Your ideas and emotions remain uncontrolled when you fail to assess your mental clutter. Your experience of existence consequently becomes erratic and wholly dependent on thought's randomness.

Your daily intrusive thoughts serve as an example of the perplexing fact that many mental processes appear to be beyond conscious control. To make matters worse, our ideas strongly influence how we perceive the outside world and feel very substantial and powerful.

For a while, let go of the idea that your unplanned thoughts have any significance. What if those bothersome thoughts are nothing more than arbitrary wall graffiti? Even while there may be a connection to an experience or an emotion, they don't accurately reflect the present. This is generally the case when it comes to thoughts.

You can control some of your thoughts, even if your subconscious mind will never let you have total control over them.

Additionally, you can alter your behaviors and responses to better control them and the associated feelings.

We've provided a wide range of suggestions and methods for clearing your mind throughout this book so you can silence the critical voice in your head, feel less stressed, and experience greater peace of mind.

You can induce relaxation and develop detachment from bothersome thoughts and emotions by practicing focused breathing and mindfulness. You can learn to control your thinking and lessen the influence thoughts have on you by interrupting, rephrasing, and disputing your thoughts.

When you establish boundaries for your decisions and activities, you prevent yourself from giving yourself more cause to reflect and worry.

You don't waste time on things that will later make you regret them or give you mental agony once you have established your life priorities.

You create the conditions for targeted action and self-esteem that keep you feeling energized when you set goals based on your beliefs and priorities.

You leave little place for negative thinking when you pursue and live your passion since it will provide authenticity, meaning, and excitement to your goals.

Being more conscious and present in your relationships helps you avoid many of the problems that arise from interpersonal interaction, reducing the resulting emotional pain and raising relationship satisfaction.

You may avoid distractions that drag you away from your beliefs, priorities, and goals by maintaining a clean, organized and streamlined environment in both your physical space and your digital life.

You can create more "space" to be present and pay attention to life by deciding to reduce the number of tasks and commitments you have. This reduces stress.

You transcend the mental chatter in your head to become one with the activity as you focus on the task at hand and engage in "flow" activities, which promote emotions of delight and deep fulfillment. You avoid the distress that results from putting things off when you confront procrastination and develop the ability to go rapidly into the initial step.

Applying mindfulness to every aspect of daily life, from exercising to doing the dishes, allows you to focus entirely on the only true reality of the moment.

How then do you choose where to start your mental clutter-clearing routine?

We advise you to start by outlining your basic beliefs, top priorities, and long-term objectives. It will be much simpler for you to identify the areas of your mind that are the most disruptive and decide how you want to deal with them once you have created these personal boundaries and directives.

The relationship activities we provided are a fantastic place to start your mental decluttering, for instance, if you have a core goal of developing solid relationships but you frequently find yourself in dispute with someone or dwelling over a previous encounter.

Or perhaps you frequently criticize your skills or appearance, and these unfavorable ideas keep you from having fun.

If so, you might want to start by working on self-acceptance, giving up comparisons, and forgiving yourself.